"To the imaginative dreamers, the curious explorers, and the boundless adventurers

– this book is lovingly dedicated to you!

IN A LITTLE TOWN CALLED SUNNYVILLE

THERE LIVED A CURIOUS AND EXCITED YOUNG BOY NAMED LIAM. HE HAD HEARD MANY STORIES ABOUT FIRST DAY BACK TO SCHOOL FROM HIS OLDER SIBLINGS AND WAS EAGER TO EXPERIENCE IT FOR HIMSELF.

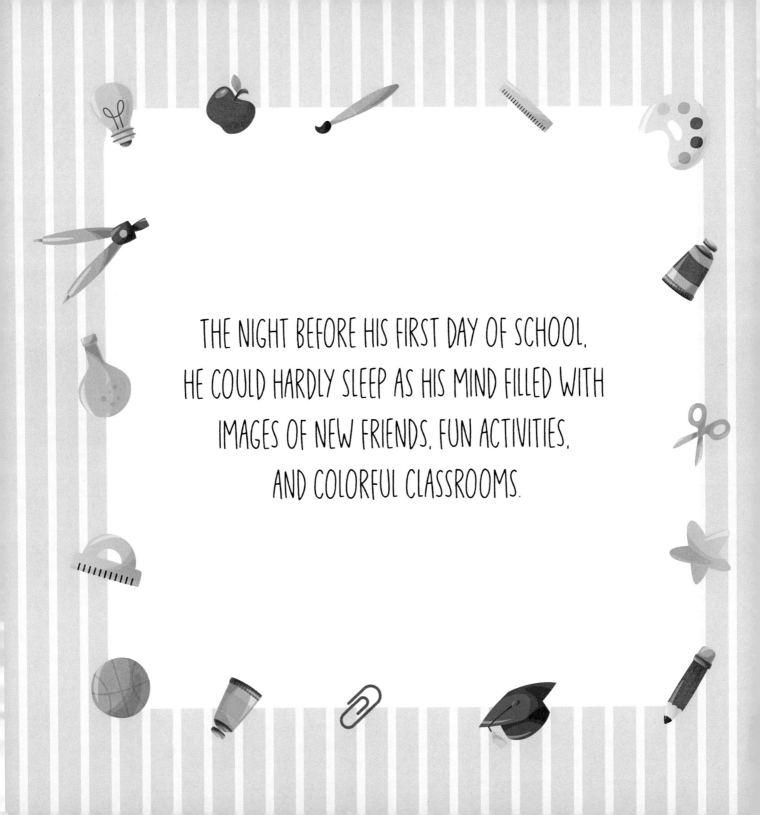

THE NIGHT BEFORE HIS FIRST DAY OF SCHOOL,
HE COULD HARDLY SLEEP AS HIS MIND FILLED WITH
IMAGES OF NEW FRIENDS, FUN ACTIVITIES,
AND COLORFUL CLASSROOMS.

THE NEXT MORNING, THE SUN ROSE EARLY,
AND SO DID LIAM, WITH HIS BACKPACK
ON HIS LITTLE SHOULDERS AND A
LUNCHBOX FILLED WITH HIS FAVORITE
SNACKS.

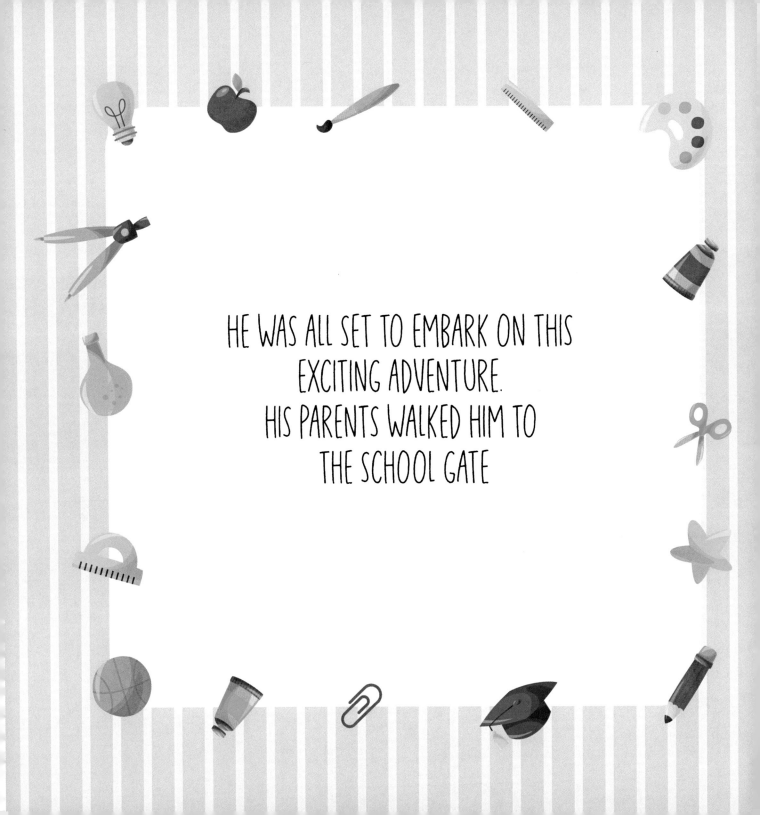

HE WAS ALL SET TO EMBARK ON THIS
EXCITING ADVENTURE.
HIS PARENTS WALKED HIM TO
THE SCHOOL GATE

As Liam entered the school building, he felt a mix of nervousness and excitement. He followed his teacher, Mrs. Taylor, into the classroom filled with bright colors and all kinds of toys and games.

THE ROOM BUZZED WITH LAUGHTER AND CHATTER
AS OTHER CHILDREN EXPLORED THE PLAY AREA.

MRS. TAYLOR INTRODUCED LIAM TO HIS NEW CLASSMATES,
AND THEY WELCOMED HIM WITH WARM SMILES. LIAM
SOON MADE A NEW FRIEND NAMED TIM, WHO HAD
THE SAME INTERESTS AS HIM. THEY QUICKLY
BECAME INSEPARABLE.

THE MORNING PASSED IN A BLUR OF EXCITING
ACTIVITIES. THEY SANG SONGS,
LISTENED TO STORIES, AND PLAYED FUN GAMES.
THEY EVEN DID SOME PAINTING AND
MADE COLORFUL ARTWORK THAT THEY
PROUDLY DISPLAYED ON THE WALLS.

AT SNACK TIME, LIAM SHARED HIS SNACKS WITH TIM,
AND TIM SHARED HIS SNACKS WITH LIAM.
THEY GIGGLED AND ENJOYED THEIR TREATS
TOGETHER, MAKING THEIR FRIENDSHIP
EVEN STRONGER.

After snack time, it was time for outdoor play. The school had a beautiful playground with swings, slides, and a sandbox. Liam and Tim ran around, climbed, and slid down the slides, laughing and shouting in delight.

AS THE DAY PROGRESSED, LIAM'S NERVOUSNESS MELTED
AWAY, AND HE FELT LIKE HE BELONGED.
HE REALIZED THAT SCHOOL WAS A PLACE
FULL OF FUN, LEARNING, AND FRIENDSHIP.
HE LOVED EVERY MOMENT OF IT.

WHEN IT WAS TIME TO GO HOME, LIAM GAVE MRS. TAYLOR A BIG HUG AND THANKED HER FOR THE WONDERFUL DAY. HE COULDN'T WAIT TO COME BACK TO SCHOOL TOMORROW.

AS LIAM AND HIS PARENTS WALKED BACK HOME,
HE CHATTED HAPPILY ABOUT ALL THE EXCITING
THINGS HE DID IN THE CLASSROOM
AND HOW HE COULDN'T WAIT TO SEE
HIS NEW FRIENDS AGAIN.

FROM THAT DAY ON, LIAM'S EXCITEMENT FOR SCHOOL ONLY GREW.

EVERY MORNING, HE EAGERLY GOT READY FOR SCHOOL, LOOKING FORWARD

TO EXPLORING, LEARNING, AND PLAYING WITH HIS FRIENDS. AND SO,

LIAM'S FIRST DAY IN SCHOOL MARKED THE BEGINNING OF A FANTASTIC

JOURNEY FILLED WITH ADVENTURES, LAUGHTER, AND MANY CHERISHED MEMORIES.